HUMAN BODY

Anna Claybourne

Illustrated by Chrissy Barnard

WAYLAND
www.waylandbooks.co.uk

First published in 2014 by Wayland

Text copyright © Wayland 2014
Illustrations © Wayland 2014

Wayland
338 Euston Road
London NW1 3BH

Wayland Australia
Level 17/207 Kent Street
Sydney, NSW 2000

Series editor: Victoria Brooker
Series designer: Lisa Peacock

A CIP catalogue record for this book is available
from the British Library.
Dewey number: 612–dc23

ISBN: 978 0 7502 8280 2
Ebook ISBN: 978 0 7502 8833 0

10 9 8 7 6 5 4 3 2 1

Printed in China

Wayland is a division of Hachette Children's Books,
an Hachette UK Company
www.hachette.co.uk

Contents

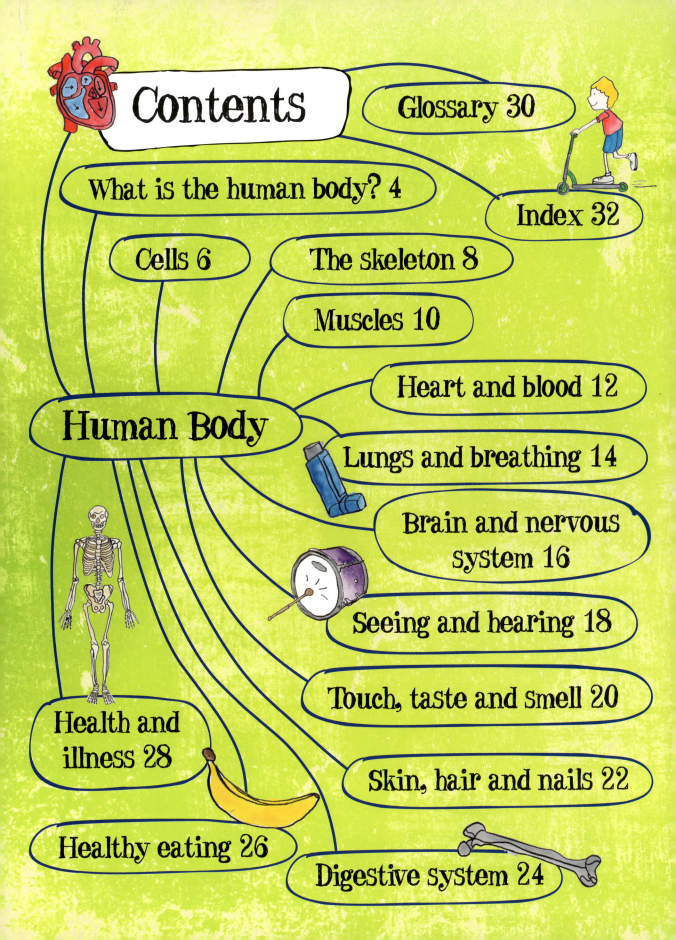

What is the human body?

You live in an amazing machine. It walks and runs, talks and sings, thinks and grows, takes in food and oxygen, and gets rid of the waste it doesn't need. It fights germs, keeps itself cool or warm, and if it gets cut or scratched, it can heal itself! In fact, it can even make new copies of itself. It's the human body – an incredibly complex and clever living thing.

Built from bits

Like other living things, the human body is made up of tiny units called cells. Most of them are far too small to see on their own. But together, they form larger body parts, such as bones, muscles, skin and blood, and organs like the brain, stomach and heart. The human body, and the cells it is made of, also contain a lot of water. A typical human is about 60% water.

Body parts also work together in groups, to form body systems. Each body system does a particular job for the body. For example, the digestive system takes food into the body and breaks it down into chemicals for the body to use. The digestive system includes the mouth, stomach and intestines. The circulatory system carries blood around the body. It includes the heart and blood vessels. This book explores the body's main systems, the organs they are made of, and how they work.

What is a mind web?

In this book, all the facts you need to know about the human body are arranged into mind webs. A mind web is a way of laying out information about a topic on a single page. The topic title goes in the middle, with all the important facts and words arranged around it. There are lines to link things together, and little pictures to help you remember things.

Mind webs are very useful for helping you think, learn and sort out ideas. They let you see a topic all at once, showing how all the parts are linked together. Because the mind web looks like a picture, your brain may also find it easier to remember. Mind webs can also be called mind maps, spidergrams or spider graphs. This mini mind web shows some of the main topics to do with the human body.

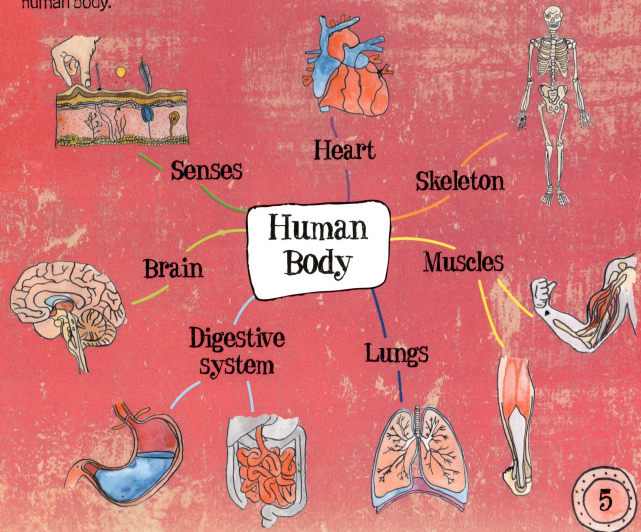

Senses

Heart

Skeleton

Brain

Human Body

Muscles

Digestive System

Lungs

control how
cells work

spiral-
shaped
chemical

found in
cell nucleus

brain

stomach

eye

organs

heart

make body
parts

give instructions
to cells

DNA

50-100 trillion
in 1 human body

Human cells

sections of DNA

genes

Genes and
DNA

liver

liver cells

Types of
human cells

Cells

rod and
cone cells

brain

nerves

neurons

muscle
cells

skin
cells

red blood
cells

white
blood cells

sense light
in the eye

muscle

skin

blood

carry oxygen

blood

fight germs

6

snot

blood

sweat

bone

skin

tissues

fluids

muscle

cell membrane (skin)

genes

nucleus

cytoplasm (watery jelly)

organelles (parts)

Parts of a cell

Reproductive cells

female reproductive cell

male reproductive cell

egg

sperm

join to make baby

Cells are the tiny parts that make up living things. They work together in groups to form all the different body parts and to keep the body working. Each cell has its own skin or cell membrane, and its own tiny parts, or organelles. Most cells have a nucleus, or control centre, containing genes. These are instructions that tell cells what to do, and control the way the body works and grows. Slight differences in genes make humans different from each other.

Human cells
The body has about 200 types of cell. For example, muscles are made of muscle cells and the brain and nerves are made of special nerve cells, or neurons. Altogether, a typical, fully grown human body is made up of around 50-100 trillion cells!

Reproduction
The human body also contains reproductive cells, whose job is to make new human beings. When male and female reproductive cells join together, they make a new cell that can grow into a baby.

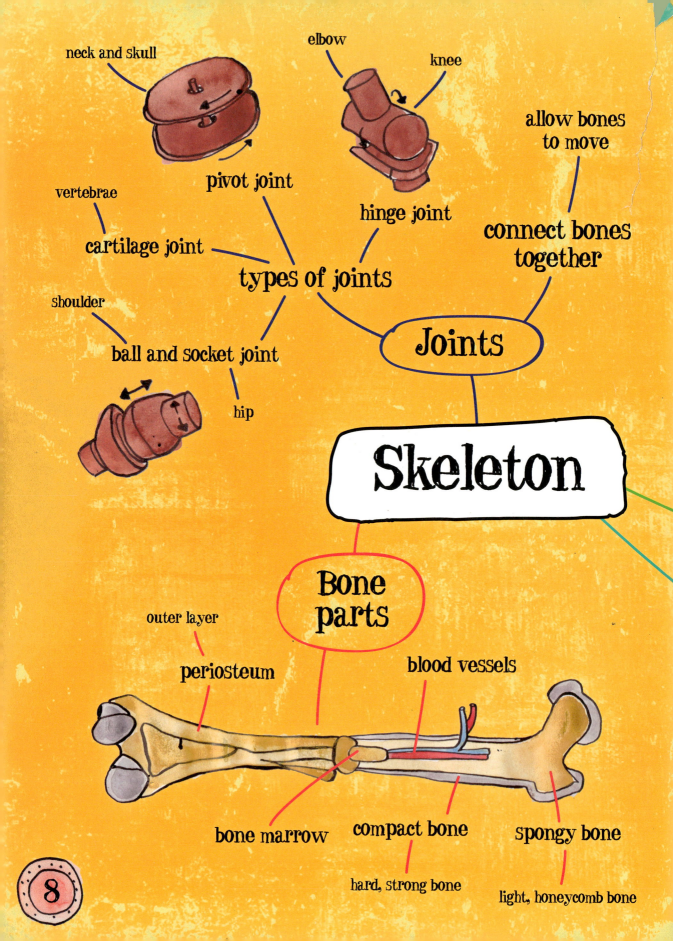

neck and skull

elbow

knee

allow bones
to move

pivot joint

vertebrae

hinge joint

connect bones
together

cartilage joint

types of joints

shoulder

ball and socket joint

Joints

hip

Skeleton

Bone
parts

outer layer

periosteum

blood vessels

bone marrow

compact bone

spongy bone

hard, strong bone

light, honeycomb bone

skull

jawbone

shoulderblade

humerus

ribs

spine or
backbone

pelvis

phalanges
(finger bones)

patella
(kneecap)

collarbone

sternum or
breastbone

ribcage

vertebrae

femur
(thigh bone)

Skeleton parts

Jobs bones do

make blood cells

hold body
up

help body
move

protect soft
organs

The skeleton

The skeleton is the framework inside your body, made up of more than 200 different bones. Your skeleton has several jobs to do. It holds your body up and gives it its shape. Parts of your skeleton, such as the skull and the ribcage, protect soft but important organs, like the brain, heart and lungs. Bones are connected together by moving joints. This means that bones can work with muscles to move your body into different positions. Bones also have another important job — they make blood cells and release them into the blood.

Inside a bone
Bones are hard, but they are not solid or dead. A typical bone has a hard outer layer or periosteum, with a layer of hard or compact bone underneath it. Inside this is lighter spongy bone that looks like a honeycomb. Large bones also contain a soft fatty substance called bone marrow, where blood cells are made.

Muscles

Muscles are a type of body tissue that your body uses to move. There are muscles all over your skeleton, attached to your bones with strong, stretchy strings called tendons. They are called skeletal muscles and you have more than 600 of them. There is also lots more muscle inside your body, known as smooth muscle. It makes organs and other body parts do the movements that make them work. For example, smooth muscle in your stomach makes it squeeze and squish food to mush it up. The heart also has to squeeze to pump blood. It's made of a special type of muscle called cardiac muscle.

Pulling

Muscles work by getting shorter, or contracting, and pulling on other body parts. Muscles can't push – they can only pull, then relax. So to move a body part such as the elbow, there are often two muscles working together. One pulls to move the elbow one way, and another pulls to move it back the other way.

attach muscles to bones

tendons in hand control fingers

achilles tendon

strong and elastic

Tendons

makes elbow straighten

contracts

triceps

another muscle pulls the other way

Pulling in pairs

makes elbow bend

contracts

biceps

one muscle pulls one way

inside muscle cells

actin

miosin

muscle filaments

relaxing

contracting

actin

miosin

attached to bones

in organs and
body parts

skeletal muscles

smooth muscles

in the heart

Types of muscle

cardiac muscles

Muscles

Main muscles

How muscles pull

pectoral

deltoid

trapezius

biceps

triceps

abdominal

contracting

relaxing

muscle gets
shorter and
pulls

muscle gets
longer

quadriceps

gluteal

calf
muscles

FRONT

BACK

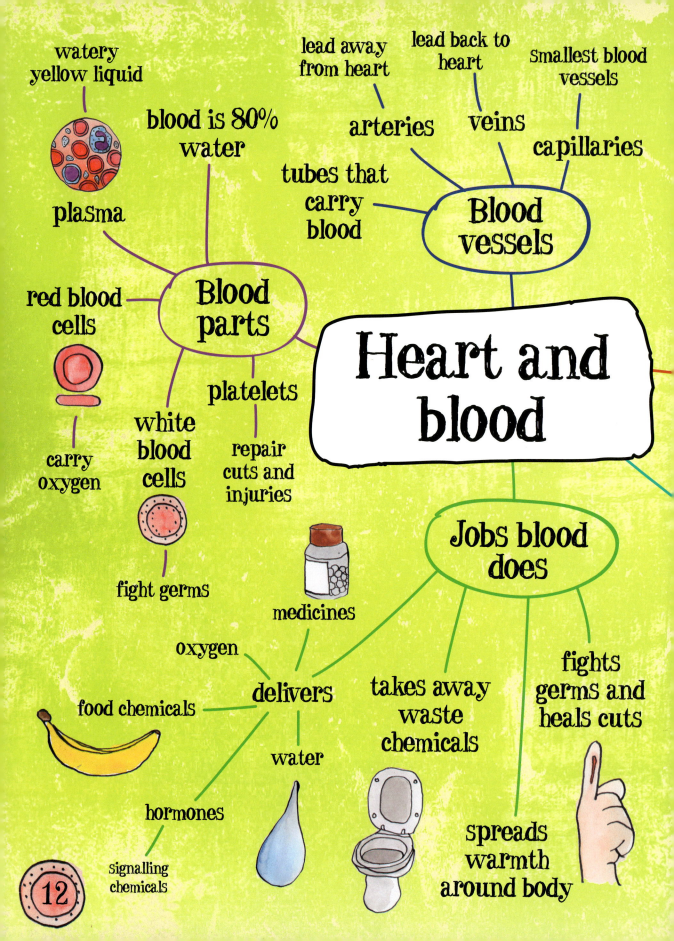

Heart and blood

Blood parts

plasma — watery yellow liquid

blood is 80% water

red blood cells — carry oxygen

white blood cells — fight germs

platelets — repair cuts and injuries

Blood vessels

tubes that carry blood

arteries — lead away from heart

veins — lead back to heart

capillaries — smallest blood vessels

Jobs blood does

delivers — oxygen, food chemicals, water, hormones, signalling chemicals, medicines

takes away waste chemicals

fights germs and heals cuts

spreads warmth around body

12

heart pushes blood out — heart muscle squeezes

heart fills with more blood — heart muscle relaxes

rhythm of heart squeezes — heart beat

pulse = number of beats per minute

How the heart works

heart rate

where is the heart?

Heart parts

arteries leading out

artery leading out

right atrium

left atrium

right ventricle

left ventricle

vein leading in

Your heart keeps working 24 hours a day, all your life. Its job is to pump blood around the body by squeezing tightly. Blood can pass through the heart in one direction only, so each time it squeezes, it pushes a bit more blood on its way around the body.

What is blood for?

Blood delivers oxygen gas to all the body's cells. Cells need a constant supply of oxygen to turn fuel into energy. Without this oxygen, muscles would stop working, and you would not be able to breathe or move. Blood collects oxygen as it flows through the lungs, then carries it to the rest of the body. Blood also carries other useful things around the body, including water, food, medicines and hormones.

Blood vessels

The heart is connected to a huge network of blood vessels that lead to all parts of the body. Vessels leading away from the heart are called arteries, and those that lead back to the heart are called veins.

Lungs and breathing

The lungs are two big, spongy organs inside your chest. They suck air into your body, extract oxygen from it and put the oxygen into your blood so that it can be delivered to all the body's cells. At the same time, the lungs collect a waste gas that the body makes, carbon dioxide, and breathe it back out. Inside the lungs, there are lots of branching passageways, leading to tiny chambers called alveoli. The alveoli are surrounded by billions of even smaller blood vessels. As you breathe in, air fills the alveoli, and the gases move into and out of the blood vessels through their walls.

Breathing bits
You breathe in and out through your nose and mouth. They are connected to the trachea or windpipe, a tube that leads to the lungs. To breathe in, muscles in your chest and under your lungs pull your lungs open, sucking air inside. To breathe out, the muscles squeeze the lungs and push air out again.

waste gas from cells

carbon dioxide

Breathing gases

turns food into energy in cells

oxygen

breathe out

Breathing muscles

breathe in

air exhaled

air inhaled

intercostal muscles make ribs contract

intercostal muscles make ribs expand

diaphragm pushes lungs up

diaphragm pulls lungs down

breathing in

extract oxygen into blood

breathing out

collect carbon dioxide out of blood

alveoli

blood vessels

How lungs work

oxygen out of alveolus

carbon dioxide into alveolus

Lungs and breathing

Lung parts

right lung

left lung

bronchus (main entrance tubes)

pleura (outer covering)

Breathing tubes

nose

mouth

throat

trachea (windpipe)

bronchi

lungs

alveoli

bronchioles (smaller tubes)

15

collect information from senses

carry signals around brain

carry signals to muscles

brain and nerve cells

sensory neurons

interneurons

motor neurons

Neurons

links brain to rest of body

Brain and nervous system

Nervous System

brain stem

spinal cord

nerves

movement

Cortex

touch

motor cortex

sensory cortex

frontal cortex

visual cortex

thinking

auditory cortex

hearing

seeing

Brain and nervous system

The brain is the control centre of your whole body. It is in charge of taking in information, deciding what to do and making it happen. It also controls a lot of other things that you don't think about, like keeping your heart beating, making you grow and breathing while you're asleep.

Your brain fills up most of your head and looks like a wobbly, wrinkly, greyish-pink jelly. It has several main parts, including the limbic system in the middle, which deals with emotions and memories, the cerebellum at the back, which controls movement, and the cortex, the brain's covering, which is where thinking happens.

Network of nerves

The cortex is made up of a huge tangle of tree-like brain cells, or neurons, that pass signals to each other. More neurons make up the nervous system, a network of pathways called nerves that connect the brain to the rest of the body. They collect information from the senses and take it to the brain. They also carry instructions from the brain to the muscles to control everything you do.

Brain jobs

thinking and understanding

making decisions

taking in information

controlling the body

learning

storing and remembering memories

Brain parts

links two sides of brain

corpus callosum

emotions

limbic system

memory

controls basic functions

brain stem

leads to body

thinking

understanding

learning

cortex

cerebellum

movement

balance

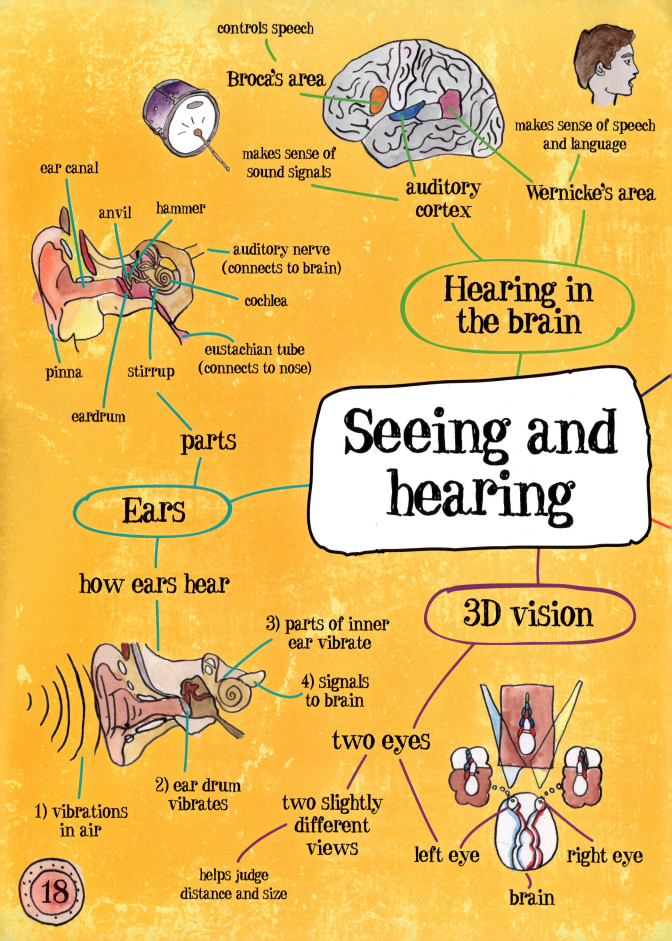

controls speech

Broca's area

makes sense of
sound signals

auditory
cortex

makes sense of speech
and language

Wernicke's area

**Hearing in
the brain**

ear canal

anvil   hammer

auditory nerve
(connects to brain)

cochlea

pinna

eardrum

stirrup

eustachian tube
(connects to nose)

parts

Ears

**Seeing and
hearing**

how ears hear

3) parts of inner
ear vibrate

4) signals
to brain

3D vision

two eyes

1) vibrations
in air

2) ear drum
vibrates

two slightly
different
views

left eye

right eye

helps judge
distance and size

brain

cornea

lens

retina

pupil

optic nerve

light entering
eye

iris

vitreous humour

parts

Eyes

how eyes see

1) object

2) light
beams

3) image on
retina

4) signals to
brain

Seeing in
the brain

visual
cortex

makes sense of light
signals

Seeing and
hearing

When you see, your eyes are collecting patterns of light from your surroundings. Light glows from light sources like lamps or the Sun, and also bounces off other objects. From here, beams of light enter your eyes. Each eye focuses the light beams onto the retina at the back of the eyeball, where they trigger light-detecting rod and cone cells. They send signals along nerves leading into the brain, where you make sense of the patterns you can see.

Hearing
Sounds happen when objects move or vibrate, setting up sound vibrations that spread out into the air. These vibrations make parts inside your ears vibrate too, and this is how you detect sounds. Deep inside each ear, the vibrations are detected by tiny hairs connected to nerves leading to the brain. The brain works out what you can hear, based on the speed and strength of the vibrations.

firm pressure

sensitive to

pain

heat

light pressure

epidermis

dermis

hypodermis

senses pressure

senses pain

touch sensor

heat and cold sensor

Skin

Touch

connect to brain

sensors in muscles and joints

Touch, taste and smell

Proprioception

senses body position

surface of
tongue

papilla

sensory
cells

taste bud

tongue

Taste

salt

sweet

sour

can
sense

bitter

Smell

umami
(savoury)

nose

3) olfactory
bulb

2) smell-
detecting
cells

1) smelly
molecules

4) connecting
to brain

Touch, taste and Smell

Smell

You smell things when molecules (tiny parts) of them float into the air and up your nose. They touch an area of smell-detecting cells inside the top of your nose, and trigger some of them. The smell signals go to your brain to tell you what you can smell – stinky socks, burnt toast or spring flowers.

Taste

You taste food when it touches your tongue and dissolves. The dissolved food flows into gaps in your tongue and touches tiny taste-sensing organs called taste buds. However, to taste things properly, you also use your sense of smell at the same time.

Touch

Your skin contains millions of nerves that can detect different kinds of touch sensation – light pressure, firm pressure, pain, heat and cold. There are also touch sensors inside your body that tell you the position your body is in. This touch sense is called proprioception.

hair shaft

sebaceous gland

oils hair

arrector pili muscle

hair bulb

hair follicle

hair papilla

Hair parts

protect fingers and toes

scratching

used as a tool

jobs nails do

Skin, hair and nails

precision grip

Nails

nail parts

Types of hair

cuticle

nail plate

bone

nail bed

head hair

body hair

direct sweat around eyes

facial hair

100,000 hairs

keeps head warm

5 million hairs

eyebrows

show facial expressions

eyelashes

keeps body warm and protected

beard

guard against dust

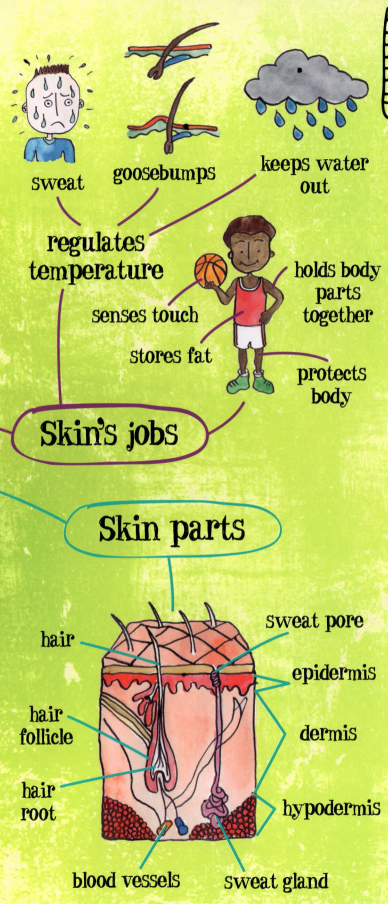

sweat

goosebumps

keeps water out

regulates temperature

senses touch

stores fat

holds body parts together

protects body

Skin's jobs

Skin parts

hair

sweat pore

epidermis

hair follicle

dermis

hair root

hypodermis

blood vessels

sweat gland

Skin, hair and nails

Your skin is one of the biggest body parts you have. It's a thick, protective covering, made up of several layers, that reaches all over and around you. Skin does several jobs. It holds all your body parts, organs, blood and blood vessels together, keeping them safely enclosed. It stops the body from drying out. but also stops water getting in when you're in the bath.

Skin contains touch-sensitive nerves (see page 20), allowing you to feel things all over your body. It releases chemicals that help to kill germs. Lastly, skin helps to keep your body at the right temperature. It releases sweat to help you cool down, and gives you goosebumps to help you warm up.

Hair and nails

Your skin is alive, except for a layer of dead cells on the surface. Nails and hair are also made of dead cells. They grow as more and more cells are gradually pushed out of your skin. Because they are dead, it doesn't hurt when you trim them!

Digestive system

The digestive system is the body system that takes in food and breaks it down so the body can use it. It's a long passageway, made up of several connected tubes and organs, that runs right through your body. Food starts off being chewed in your mouth, then swallowed. It passes down the oesophagus into the stomach, where it gets mushed up into liquid. Then it flows through the small intestine, where food chemicals are soaked up into the blood. Finally, the leftovers enter the large intestine, where they collect into lumps of waste, or faeces (poo).

Extra organs

The digestive system also includes the liver, gall bladder and pancreas. They release body substances that flow into the intestines to help digest food.

Waste water

Your body also has two kidneys that collect waste chemicals and liquid from your blood. This liquid waste is called urine, or wee. It is stored in the bladder and leaves the body through a tube called the urethra.

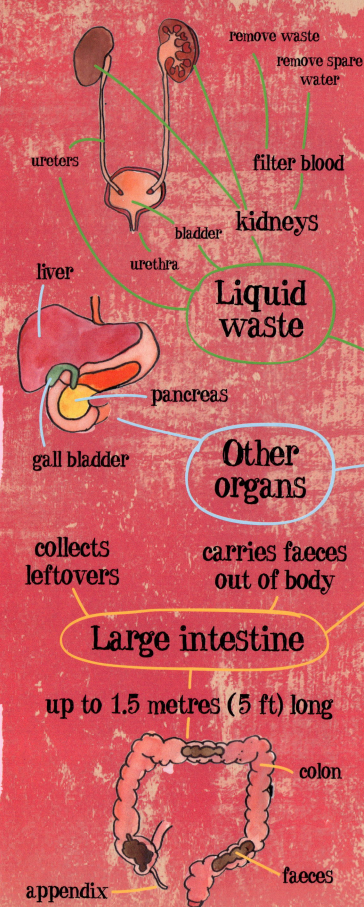

remove waste

remove spare water

filter blood

ureters

kidneys

bladder

urethra

liver

Liquid waste

pancreas

gall bladder

Other organs

collects leftovers

carries faeces out of body

Large intestine

up to 1.5 metres (5 ft) long

colon

faeces

appendix

molars
chew/grind food

canines
grip and cut food

tongue

teeth

saliva
(spit)

throat

to stomach

oesophagus

swallow food

incisors
bite food

TONGUE

Chewing and swallowing

Digestive system

Stomach

fundus
(top end)

pylorus
(bottom end)

muscles
squeeze
food

liquid

Small intestine

up to 6 metres
(20 ft) long

lined with villi

small intestines

villi

circular folds

pass into blood

soak up food
chemicals

Healthy eating

Food is the body's fuel. It gives all our cells the energy they need to work, so that they can do things like making muscles move, sending signals to and from the brain or attacking germs. Our bodies also use chemicals from food to grow, repair injuries and make body substances. We have to eat a balanced diet, containing a wide range of different foods, to get all the chemicals the body needs.

Types of food
There are several main types of food that do different jobs in the body. Carbohydrates, including sugar, provide energy. Proteins help us build and repair body parts. Fats contain energy and also help to protect organs, fight diseases and make nerves work. The body also needs small amounts of vitamins, minerals and trace elements, such as iron, zinc and Vitamin C.

Water
All the body's cells need water to work, and it's also an important part of blood, sweat, and saliva. We need plenty of water (or drinks that are mostly made of water) every day.

crisps

dairy

fruit and veg

good for teeth

bad for teeth

fizzy drinks

sweets

Healthy teeth

help cells to work

Water

saliva

used to make

blood

sweat

tears

iron

trace elements

minerals

zinc

copper

sodium

calcium

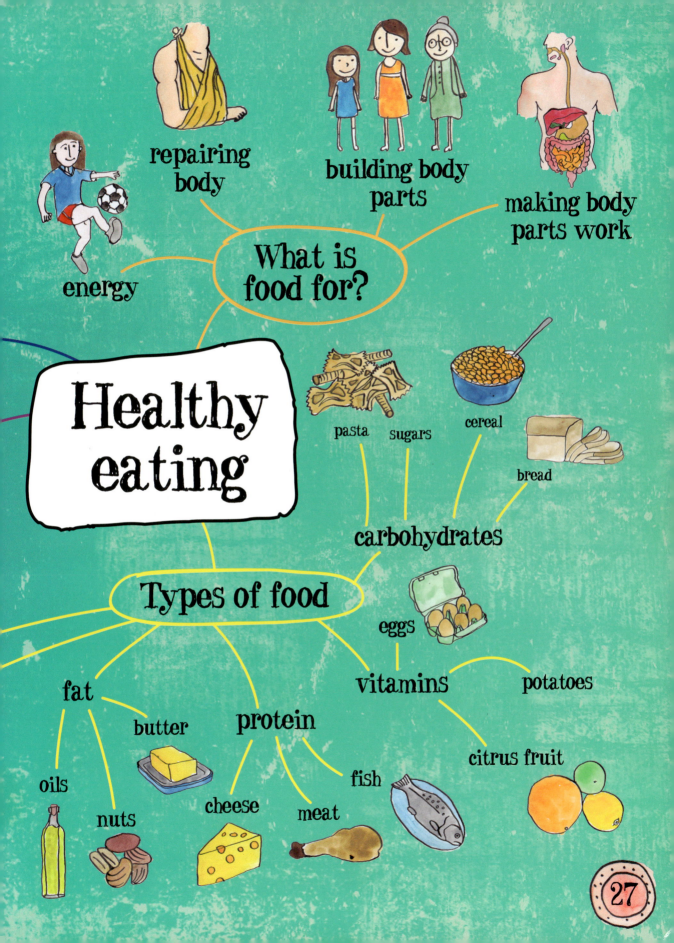

repairing body

building body parts

making body parts work

energy

What is food for?

Healthy eating

pasta   sugars   cereal

bread

carbohydrates

Types of food

eggs

vitamins   potatoes

fat

butter   **protein**

citrus fruit

oils

nuts   cheese   meat   fish

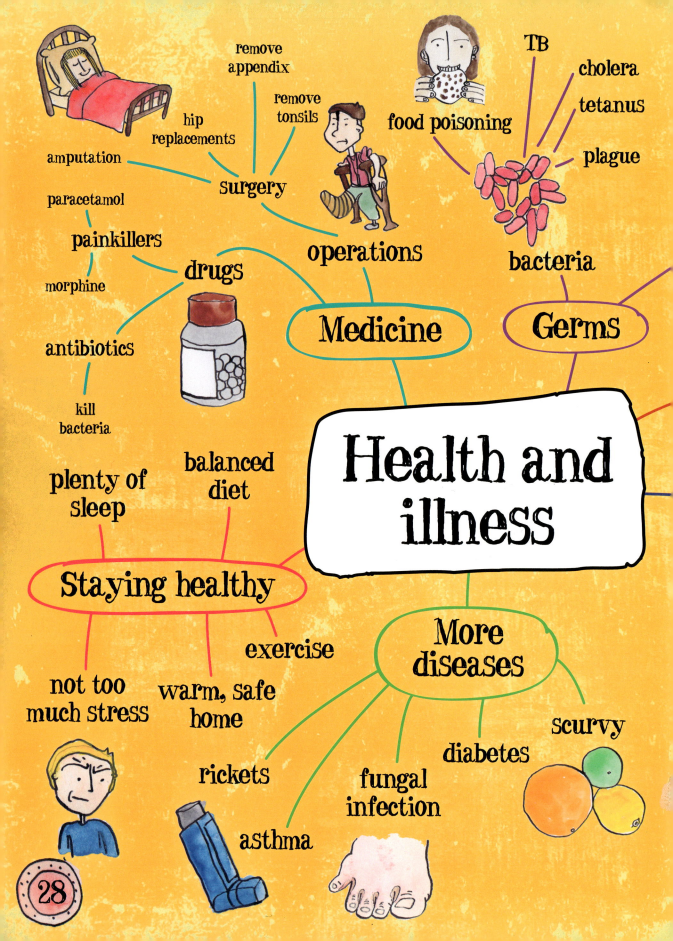

remove appendix

remove tonsils

hip replacements

amputation

surgery

paracetamol

painkillers

morphine

drugs

antibiotics

kill bacteria

operations

TB

cholera

tetanus

food poisoning

plague

bacteria

Medicine

Germs

Health and illness

balanced diet

plenty of sleep

Staying healthy

exercise

More diseases

not too much stress

warm, safe home

scurvy

diabetes

rickets

fungal infection

asthma

28

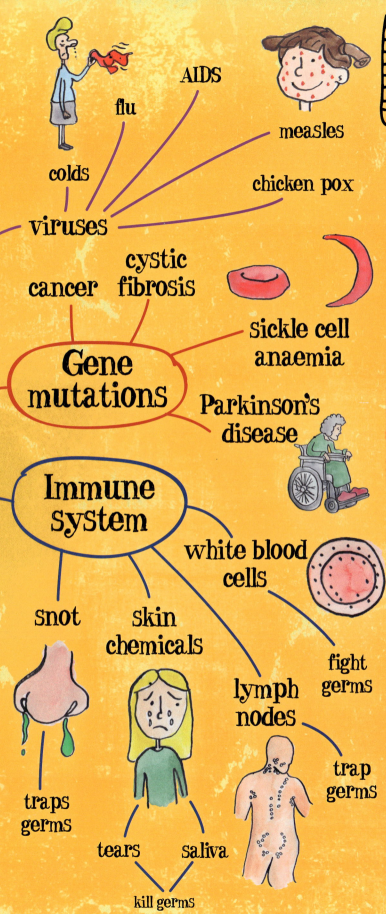

flu

AIDS

colds

measles

chicken pox

viruses

cystic
fibrosis

cancer

Sickle cell
anaemia

Gene
mutations

Parkinson's
disease

Immune
system

white blood
cells

snot

skin
chemicals

fight
germs

lymph
nodes

traps
germs

trap
germs

tears

saliva

kill germs

Health and
illness

A healthy human body is
one that has nothing wrong
with it and is working well.
But the body can go wrong
and become ill or sick. Some
illnesses are caused by germs
getting into the body. For
example, bacteria such as
Salmonella can cause food
poisoning, and colds are caused
by tiny germs called viruses.
Other germs cause diseases
like malaria, tuberculosis (TB)
and measles.

Some diseases, such as
cystic fibrosis and some
types of cancer, are caused
by mutations or problems in
a person's genes. Some are
caused by an unhealthy lifestyle
or surroundings – for example,
a lack of sunlight can give you
rickets, and not enough
Vitamin C causes scurvy.

Fighting disease
A body system called the
immune system fights germs
and diseases. It includes white
blood cells that attack germs,
and chemicals in tears, saliva
and stomach acid that
kill germs.

Glossary

alveoli Tiny chambers in the lungs that extract oxygen from the air.

arteries Blood vessels that lead away from the heart.

bacteria Germs that can cause some types of diseases.

blood vessels Tubes that carry blood around the body.

body system Group of organs and body parts that work together to do a job in the body.

bone marrow Soft substance found inside some bones.

carbohydrate A type of food that gives the body energy.

cardiac muscle A type of muscle found in the heart.

cell membrane Outer covering or skin of a cell.

cells Very small units that living things are made up of.

cerebellum Area at the back of the brain, used to control movement and balance.

compact bone Hard, solid type of bone.

cortex Wrinkled covering of the brain, used for thinking and understanding.

cytoplasm Jelly-like fluid inside a cell.

faeces Poo.

gall bladder Small organ that stores chemicals that help the body digest food.

genes Instructions found inside the nucleus of cells that control how cells work.

hormones Chemicals used by the body to send signals between body parts.

intestines Tubes that soak up chemicals from food and collect unwanted waste.

kidneys Two organs that filter the blood and remove waste chemicals and spare water.

limbic system Part of the brain that deals with emotions and memories.

liver Large organ that helps to digest food and stores useful chemicals.

minerals Non-living substances such as calcium that the body needs in order to work.

nerves Pathways that carry signals between the brain and the body.

neurons Cells that make up the brain and nerves.

nucleus The control centre of a cell.

oesophagus Tube leading from the throat into the stomach.

organelles Tiny organ-like parts inside cells.

organs Body parts that do a particular job, such as the brain and stomach.

oxygen Gas found in the air that cells need in order to work.

pancreas Small organ that helps the body digest food.

periosteum Tough outer covering of a bone.

proprioception Sense of where the body is and the position it is in.

protein A type of food the body uses to grow, make body substances and repair injuries.

retina Layer at the back of the eyeball that senses light.

skeletal muscles Muscles that are attached to bones and make them move.

smooth muscle A type of muscle found in body organs and tissues.

spongy bone Light, honeycomb-like bone found inside some bones.

taste buds Tiny taste-sensing organs found in the tongue.

tendon Strong, stretchy cord that attaches a muscle to a bone.

trace elements Substances in food that the body needs tiny amounts of.

trachea Tube leading from the throat to the lungs.

urethra Tube that carries urine (wee) from the bladder out of the body.

urine Wee.

veins Blood vessels that lead towards the heart.

virus Tiny germ that can cause some types of diseases.

vitamins Chemicals that the body needs small amounts of in order to work.

windpipe Another name for the trachea.

Index

Titles in the series:

978-0-7502-8462-2

978-0-7502-8277-2

978-0-7502-8280-2

978-0-7502-8463-9

978-0-7502-8279-6

978-0-7502-8278-9

WAYLAND

www.waylandbooks.co.uk